PATCHWORK
CROCHET

KRISTEL SALGAROLLO

D&C
David and Charles

www.stitchcraftcreate.co.uk

Contents

A note from the author
To our grandmother

My grandmother was a very independent, creative lady, who was passionate about needlecrafts. Often struggling to make ends meet, she used and re-used anything she could, always managing to create something from nothing. In fact, she was years ahead of her time when it came to recycling, and she also had a certain tendency towards rather eccentric clothing!

As the proverb goes 'the apple doesn't fall far from the tree' and of her three granddaughters (my sisters and myself), two share her love for needlecrafts, even making a living from it, while the third is a painter.

One of her great-granddaughters has also inherited her immoderate love of fashion and is likely to carry on this family tradition after her aunts.

For me, it all started at a very young age. I was only six years old when I realized what could be created with a simple hook and some yarn, thanks to a classmate and her amazing lilac and mint green sweater, which I just couldn't take my eyes off. Fascinated by these crocheted motifs, I still didn't take the needlework classes offered at school because the projects seemed too boring.

At age fourteen years, I started to crochet all kinds of tunics for my friends. I worked without a pattern, working as inspiration took me, a little bit like my grandmother. But none of this came as much of a surprise at the beginning of the seventies, with flower power in full swing.

During my last year of school, I made a full blanket of granny squares during maths classes. School had finally helped me progress in needlecrafts. Sitting in the back row, I crocheted very discreetly with my work on my knee.

Of course, my results in the end of year exams were not exactly outstanding and my teacher, Mr. Van den Bossche, said I wouldn't go far in life. He would be certainly happy to learn that I've managed to make something of myself with the little knowledge that he managed to convey to me in spite of myself on the subjects of logarithms and integrals.

So now you know all about, or almost all about, how I got started with crochet and how I have never stopped. I always have a work in progress, which I carry with me in my car, on the train or in the waiting rooms that have now replaced maths class. It's one of the great advantages and pleasures of this technique.

When six years ago I decided to offer yarn and cotton in my store, I had no doubt that knitting and crochet would experience a resurgence in popularity and once again capture the hearts of young mothers and stylish women.

Many of you know me thanks to patchwork, and I hope to continue with this and crochet for a long time to come (as well as all the rest!), I am never short of ideas and I already have enough to keep me busy for the next hundred or so years!

I am delighted to share this personal history with you and hope that you will enjoy creating the pieces in this book.

Finally, I would like to say a big thank you to my sister Inez, who has been kind enough to transform the grandma's garden design into a real blanket by patiently crocheting the countless small hexagons and sewing in all the yarn.

Kristel Salgarollo

Guide to using crochet charts

The instructions for each of the designs in this book are written in the form of a chart. This is a visual representation of how the motifs look when completed. Each stitch is drawn and it is easy to see where it should be worked.

For pieces worked in rows, the diagrams are read from the bottom to the top, with the foundation chain on the bottom edge. For those motifs worked out from a ring, the foundation ring will be in the centre of the chart. Each round or row is numbered.

Each type of stitch is represented by a different symbol. This symbol shows the height of the stitch, so the symbol for a double crochet is shorter than that for a treble. Use the symbol key below to see what each symbol means. The same motif is used to represent the most commonly used stitches in every diagram. Special or unusual stitches have their own emblems, but similar symbols may

mean slightly different things in different diagrams, so always check the key to make sure you work the stitch correctly. Stitches, such as clusters or popcorns, are drawn as they appear when you crochet them.

The charts also show where motifs are joined to each other, either in crochet as they are worked, or by oversewing.

For the 3-D designs, such as Nine Squares and Flowers in Relief, the first two rounds that make up the flower are drawn on a separate diagram. Background motifs are joined to the flowers in the four corresponding places marked with a star. Then, the motif continues as drawn on the separate diagram.

Borders are worked at the end, and a diagram showing part of each border is drawn – repeat the stitch as shown all the way around the throw or cushion.

Yarn weights

You will see that generally, a specific yarn weight or type is not provided. This is so that you can decide what type of yarn you wish to use to make each project. However, if you want some guidance on what to use, the hook size provided in the 'You will need list' gives an indication of which hook measurement is suitable. Then compare this with the hook size specified on the ball band of the yarn you'd like to use. If your band gives a larger hook size, the motifs will end up being larger than those in the book.

Symbol key

⬭	Chain
⬬	Slip stitch
✕	Double crochet
T	Half-treble
↑	Treble
‡	Double treble

Basics of crochet

How to make a cushion cover

Note: dimensions are given without seam allowances. Provide for a seam allowance of 1cm (½in) all the way around, except for the sides with hems.

For the **Front**, cut a rectangle (or square) of fabric matching the width (= a) and height (= b) of the cushion.

For the **Back**, cut two rectangles the same width as the front. The height of the first one should be ½b, + 1.5cm (½in) (for the hem), and the second should be ½b, + 4.5cm (1¾in), which will create an overlap of 3cm (1¼in) and allow 1.5cm (⅝in) for the hem.

Make a double fold (the first of 0.5cm (¼in) and the second of 1cm (½in) along the edge that will be at the centre back of the cushion and stitch. Do the same with the second half-back.

Place the front and the half-backs (the latter will overlap by 3cm (1¼in)), right side to right side, and sew all around. Turn over.

Sew the crocheted part to the front using invisible stitches.

Tip: the larger the piece is, the larger the overlap between the two half-backs should be. It is therefore recommended that you alter this overlap depending on the size of the cushion.

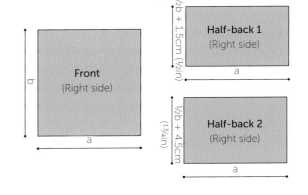

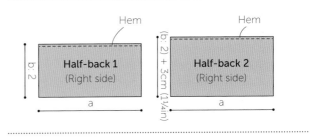

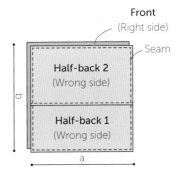

INSTRUCTIONS FOR MAKING THE PIECES

For work made from motifs assembled together, each motif requires only a small quantity of yarn. It is possible to change the colour of yarn and dimensions of the pieces to change their uses.

1. The quantity of yarn, dimensions and samples are approximate. Depending on the tension of the yarn, measurements are likely to differ slightly.

2. After completing a crocheted motif, compare its dimensions with the samples. If they match, the finished item will be with the size indicated. If they are larger, use a smaller hook, or if they are smaller, work with a larger hook.

3. See Additional methods before starting.

Basic crochet techniques and symbols

Slip knot

Step 1: place the hook behind the yarn and turn, following the arrow.

Step 2: hold the loop obtained using the thumb.

Step 3: pull one loop through the other.

Step 4: pull the end of the yarn downwards in order to tighten the loop that has just been formed.

Step 5: the 1st loop is complete.

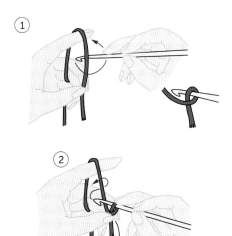

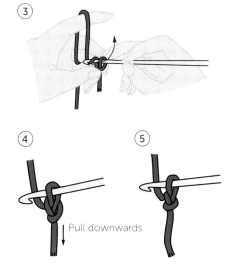

Support with the thumb

Pull downwards

⬭ Chain

Step 1: yarn over the hook, taking the yarn in the direction of the arrow.

Step 2: pull the loop through the base loop to make the 1st chain.

Step 3: pull through the next loop to make the 2nd chain.

Step 4: repeat.

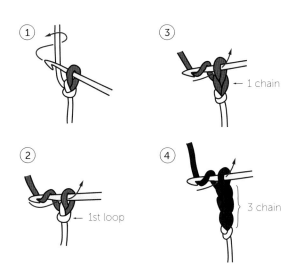

← 1 chain

← 1st loop

3 chain

Slip stitch

Step 1: at the beginning of the row, insert the hook in the 1st stitch, as shown by the arrow.

Step 2: yarn over hook, pull the yarn through the stitch and through the loop on the hook – one loop remains.

Step 3: insert the hook in the 2nd stitch, as shown by the arrow.

Step 4: this stitch tends to be quite tight, so it is advisable to crochet quite loosely (= lengthen the loop slightly).

☒ Double crochet

Step 1: 1 chain to turn, then insert the hook as shown in the diagram.

Step 2: Yarn over and pull the yarn through the loop following the arrow. Two loops on the hook.

Step 3: Yarn over and pull the yarn through both loops on the hook.

Step 4: 1 dc is completed. Repeat steps 1 to 3.

Step 5: 3 dc are completed.

1 chain to turn

Base chain

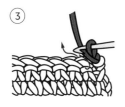

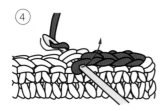

⊤ Half-treble

Step 1: start with 2 chains that replace the first half-treble. Insert the hook in the back loop of the 4th ch, counting from the hook.

Step 2: yarn over hook, pull the hook back through the loop, yarn over hook again and pull back through all the loops on the hook.

Step 3: 1 htr is completed. Repeat steps 1 and 2.

Step 4: 4 htr are crocheted (2 chain which replace the 1st htr and 3 htr).

2 chain to replace the 1st htr

Base chain

⊤ Treble

Step 1: start with 3 chains (which make the 1st treble). Then, yarn over hook and insert the hook in the 5th chain from the hook.

Step 2: yarn over hook, pull it through the stitch, following the arrow.

Step 3: yarn over hook, pull it back through the first 2 loops on the hook.

Step 4: yarn over hook and pull through the remaining 2 loops on the hook.

Step 5: repeat steps 1 to 4. 4 trebles are crocheted (3 chains which replace the 1st tr and 3 tr.).

3 chains to replace the 1st tr.

Base chain

Double treble

Turning chain in blue

Step 1: 4 ch to replace 1st dtr, then yarn over hook twice and insert the hook at the place specified by the arrow.

Step 2: yarn over hook and pull it back through the loop. Yarn over once more and pull through 2 loops.

Step 3: yarn over once more and pull through 2 loops.

Step 4: yarn over once more and pull through the last loops on the hook.

Step 5: 1 dtr is completed. Repeat steps 1 to 4.

Step 6: 4 dtr are crocheted (4 chains which replace the 1st dtr and 3 dtr).

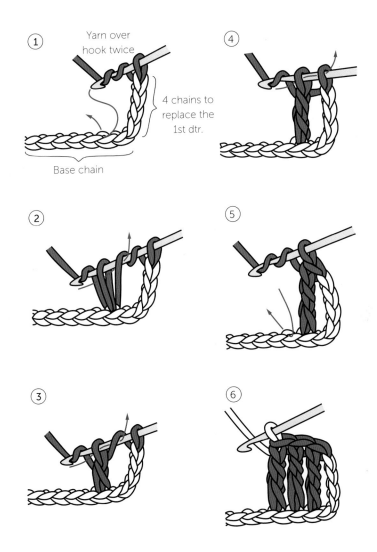

For double crochet, half-treble, treble and double treble stitches, I like to insert the hook into the back loop of the chain stitches made in the foundation chain. If you are used to inserting your hook through the 'v' on top of the stitches in the foundation chain, then this will also work.

Turning chain

At the beginning of each row, the 1st stitch must be replaced by a turning chain made up of the equivalent number of chain stitches (except for the slip stitch). The diagrams below show the number of chain stitches needed to replace each stitch.

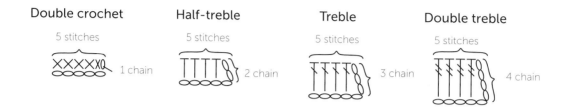

Double crochet	Half-treble	Treble	Double treble
5 stitches	5 stitches	5 stitches	5 stitches
1 chain	2 chain	3 chain	4 chain

Starting a piece crocheted in the round

There are two techniques:

Magic Loop

Step 1: wind the yarn twice around the index finger, insert the hook through the loops.
Step 2: yarn over hook, and pull the loop through the ring.
Step 3: holding the hook over the top of the ring, yarn over and pull it through the loop on the hook. The round is completed.

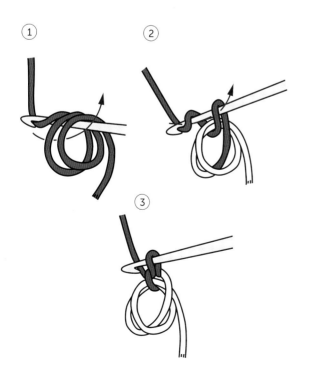

Round created with a chain

Step 1: work the required number of chains (in this case 10 ch), insert the hook in the 1st ch.

Step 2: 1 sl s. The round is completed.

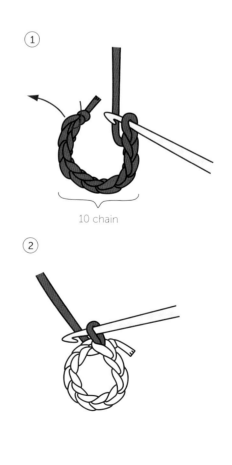

10 chain

Additional methods

Changing yarn colours

There are two main ways of changing colours. Choose based on the finish you want to achieve.

Basic

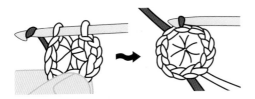

Before crocheting the last sl st of the round, yarn over with the new colour yarn and pull this loop through both loops on the hook.

The yarn colour is changed from the beginning of the next rnd.

Variation

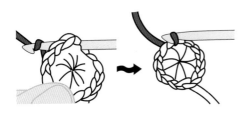

Crochet the last sl s and fasten off your first colour. Attach the new yarn by inserting the hook into a stitch and drawing the yarn through, then begin to crochet the 2nd round. This technique makes it possible to change the location of the beginning of the round and will make the stitches look uniform by working under both strands of the stitch from the previous round.

Assembling motifs by oversewing

This technique is appropriate for geometric motifs, such as squares or hexagons.

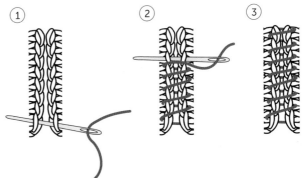

Step 1: Place 2 motifs side by side. Insert the darning needle into the corresponding stitches of the last row you crocheted.

Step 2: Assemble the motifs by stitching each edge stitch together with its corresponding stitch on the other square.

Step 3: When the two edges are fully attached, continue to join the other motifs in the same way.

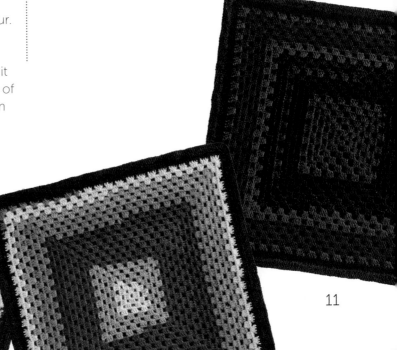

13

Hourglasses and windmills

Composed of triangles assembled in squares, this rather quaint throw in the colours of the four seasons is perfectly on trend.

You will need:

- 100g (3½oz) of yarn in the following colours: burgundy, brown, ecru, khaki, lime green, dark khaki, orange, red, mustard, beige and dark brown
- 3.5mm hook

Sample

1 square motif = 11 x 11cm (4¼ x 4¼in)

Dimensions

See diagram

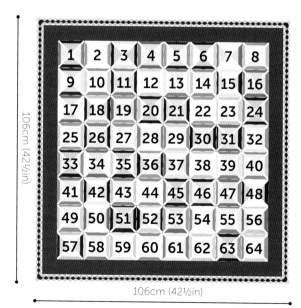

106cm (42½in)

106cm (42½in)

To make

1. Start with a magic loop. Crochet hourglass **a** (see pink section below).

2. Starting from hourglass **b**, join the last round to the previous motif using double crochet as shown in the diagram. Work hourglasses **c** and **d**, joining each one to the previous motif. You will end up with a square.

3. For colours, see Sequence of colours.

4. Crochet the square motifs according to the numerical order on the drawing on the previous page.

Square motif

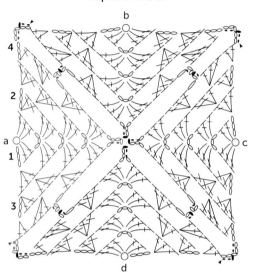

❖   See Additional methods for how to change colours

◄ Cut yarn   ◁ Attach yarn

Assembling the squares

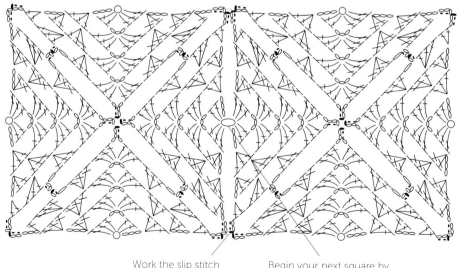

Work the slip stitch through the arch of the adjacent motif.

Begin your next square by working into the base and loop of the previous motif.

5. For the **border**, work 7 rounds of treble crochet in dark brown, 1 round of shell stitich in beige, 1 round of shell stitich in burgundy and 1 round of shell stitich in mustard, as shown in the diagram.

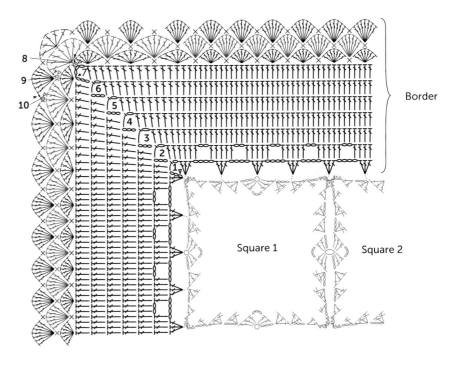

Border

Square 1

Square 2

Sequence of colours

Square no.	a and c motifs	b and d motifs
1 and 45	brown	burgundy
2	khaki	ecru
3	burgundy	lime green
4 and 47	orange	dark khaki
5	khaki	red
6 and 35	mustard	burgundy
7 and 50	dark khaki	ecru
8	beige	khaki
9	lime green	red
10 and 49	mustard	orange
11 and 26	red	brown
12	ecru	mustard
13, 39 and 55	lime green	brown
14	beige	orange
15 and 42	red	lime green
16	brown	dark khaki
17 and 34	ecru	dark khaki
18	burgundy	beige
19	dark khaki	khaki
20	beige	burgundy
21 and 31	red	dark khaki
22	ecru	khaki
23 and 62	mustard	beige
24 and 33	orange	burgundy
25	mustard	khaki

Square no.	a and c motifs	b and d motifs
27	lime green	orange
28	brown	ecru
29 and 64	orange	mustard
30	burgundy	brown
32	khaki	lime green
36	red	khaki
37	dark khaki	lime green
38	ecru	beige
40 and 49	orange	mustard
41	khaki	brown
43	beige	brown
44 and 60	ecru	orange
46	mustard	red
48	burgundy	ecru
51	burgundy	red
52	red	mustard
53	khaki	dark khaki
54	orange	ecru
56	dark khaki	beige
57	red	beige
58	mustard	brown
59	beige	lime green
61	brown	lime green
63	khaki	burgundy

Flowers
and twists

With its border of folded polka-dot material, a subtly textured white centre panel and appliquéd flowers, this throw is a reminder of times gone by.

You will need:

- 400g (14oz) of ecru yarn
- Small amounts of cotton in the following colours: red, burgundy, raspberry, fuchsia, coral, yellow, orange, copper, pale green, green and dark green
- 108 x 133cm (43 x 53in) of red fabric with white spots
- 89 x 114cm (35½ x 45½in) of fleece
- Red embroidery thread, green quilting cotton thread
- 3.5mm hook

Sample

1 motif x 7 rows = 7 x 7cm (2¾ x 2¾in)

Dimensions

See diagram

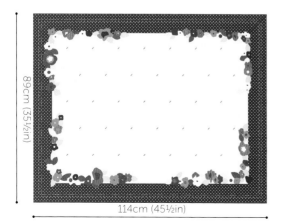

89cm (35½in)

114cm (45½in)

To make

1. For the **centre panel**, start by making a foundation chain of 208 ch in ecru, then work 74 rows of the special stitch as shown in the diagram below. You will obtain a rectangle of 69 x 95cm (27½ x 38in).

Special stitch

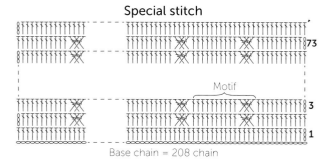

Base chain = 208 chain

"Twist": skip 2 stitches, 1 dtr in 3rd stitch and 1 dtr in 4th stitch of previous row, then work 1 dtr in 1st stitch and 1 dtr in the 2nd stitch.

2. Centre the wrong side of the crocheted panel on the right side of the fleece and sew the two layers together. Then place this piece, with the right side facing outwards, on the wrong side of the fabric, and tack (baste). Fold the fabric to obtain a size of 89 x 114cm (35¾ x 45½in) by following the diagrams below.

3. With the red embroidery thread, make knots on the back (bringing the thread through all of the layers) spaced at 10cm (4in) apart. Then quilt two straight green lines on the borders with green thread (see photo opposite).

4. Make 63 leaves and 65 flowers following the charts opposite, varying the shapes and colours according to your preference.
Note: leave some yarn for assembly.

5. Arrange the leaves and flowers in a garland around the edge of the crocheted panel (see photo opposite for inspiration) and attach by sewing in the centre of the flowers and along the middle of the leaves, being careful to ensure your stitches do not appear on the other side of the fabric.

Author's note: for flowers, I referred to 100 Flowers to Knit and Crochet *by Lesley Stanfield.*

Assembly with folded edges

Place the base section + fleece (right side facing outwards) in the centre of the fabric (wrong side facing outwards) and tack (baste). Then turn down the edge of the fabric by 0.5cm (¼in) all around.

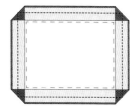

Fold the corners of the fabric over the sides. Then fold in both sides and the top and bottom, following the dotted lines, to create the sides of the base section.

Sew the sides (including the corners and mitres) with invisible stitches. Remove the tacking.

Flower 1

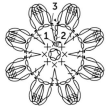

Flower 2

Flower 3

Flower 4

Flower 5

Flower 6

Leaf 1

Base chain = 7 chain

Leaf 2

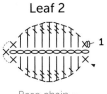

Base chain = 11 chain

◀   Cut yarn

Popcorn of 4 dtr: work 4 dtr, stretch the loop a little from the hook and take the hook out of the work. Then insert it from front to back in the top of the 1st of the 4 double trebles, pick up the loop and pull it through the stitch

2 treble cluster: work 2 incomplete tr. (leaving the last loop on the hook). Pull yarn through the last 3 loops at once

2 double treble cluster: work 2 incomplete d tr. (leaving the last loop on the hook). Pull yarn through the last 3 loops at once

3 treble cluster: work 3 incomplete tr. (leaving the last loop on the hook). Pull yarn through the last 4 loops at once

Multi-coloured stripes

Row after row, unfold waves of deep colour and use this throw to become an expert at chevron stitch.

You will need:

- 125g (4½oz) of yarn in the following colours: light blue, beige, slate, blue-grey, light khaki, off-white, mauve, burgundy, lime green, fuchsia, midnight blue and blue
- 50g (1¾oz) of yarn (or cotton) raspberry
- 3.5mm hook

Sample

1 motif x 7 rows = 10 x 10cm (4 x 4in)

Dimensions

See diagram

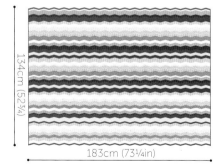

134cm (52¾in)

183cm (73¼in)

To make

1. Start with a foundation chain of 604 ch and work in chevron stitch (see diagram).

2. For stripe sequence, see Sequence of colours below. For colour changes, see Additional methods.

3. For the **border**, work 1 round of trebles in raspberry as shown in the diagram (right).

❖ For colour changes, see Additional methods, and work directly to the relevant stitch (without working a dc).

◀ Cut yarn

◁ Attach yarn

Chevron stitch

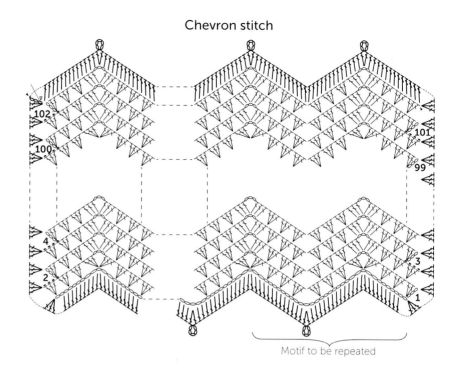

Motif to be repeated

Sequence of colours

1st–2nd row, 25th–26th row, 50th row, 74th–75th row, 102nd row	light blue
3rd–4th row, 29th row, 54th–55th row, 79th–80th row	beige
5th–6th row, 27th–28th row, 51st–53rd row, 76th–78th row	slate
7th–8th row, 30th–31st row, 56th–57th row, 81st–82nd row	blue-grey
9th–11th row, 32nd–33rd row, 58th row, 83rd–85th row	light khaki

12th–13th row, 34th–36th row, 59th–60th row, 86th–87th row	off-white
14th–15th row, 37th–38th row, 61st–63rd row, 88th–89th row	mauve
16th row, 39th–41st row, 64th row, 90th–92nd row	burgundy
17th–19th row, 42nd–43rd row, 65t–66th row, 93rd–94th row	lime green
20th–21st row, 44th–45th row, 67th–68th row, 95th–96th row	fuchsia
22nd row, 46th–47th row, 69th–71st row, 97th–98th row	midnight blue
23rd–24th row, 48th–49th row, 72th-73rd row, 99th-101st row	blue

Rainbow chevrons

This gorgeous throw is made by combining knitting and crochet to create a soft, iridescent piece, ideal for hanging over a bed.

You will need:

- 250g (9oz) of grey yarn
- 25g (1oz) of yarn in the following colours: lime green, light green, light beige, beige, yellow, orange, dark orange, old rose, red and raspberry
- 5mm hook
- 5mm knitting needles

Sample

1 motif x 9 rows of crochet = 12 x 10cm (5 x 4in)
16 stitches x 18 rows with knitting needles = 10 x 10cm (4 x 4in)

Dimensions

See diagram

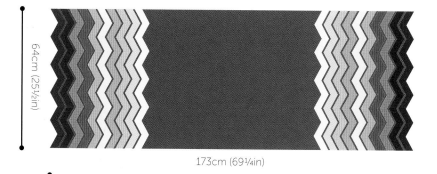

64cm (25½in)

173cm (69¼in)

To make

1. Crochet a foundation chain of 44 ch, then work 32 rows in chevron stitch (see diagram).

2. For stripe sequence, see Sequence of colours below.

Chevron stitch

Motif to be repeated

Sequence of colours

1st–2nd row	raspberry
3rd, 6th, 9th, 12th, 15th,	beige
18th, 21st, 24th, 27th 30th, 31st, 32nd row	grey
4th–5th row	red
7th–8th row	old rose
10th–11th row	dark orange
13th–14th row	orange
16th–17th row	yellow
19th–20th row	beige
22nd–23rd row	light beige
25th–26th row	light green
28th–29th row	lime green

❖   See Additional methods for how to change colours

◀   Cut yarn   △   Attach yarn

3. With knitting needles and using grey, pick up 44 stitches from the crochet section and knit in stocking stitch for 92cm (36¾in) (1st row: knit all stitches, 2nd row: purl all stitches). Repeat these two rows). Cast off all stitches.

4. With the hook, pick up 44 stitches from the knitted section and work another 32 rows of chevron stitch, reversing the colour sequence used at the start.

5. You will need to block your knitting to help it lie flat where it meets the crocheted chevron section. Do this by wetting it, pinning it out to the correct shape and leaving it to dry. Or alternatively, pin it out to the correct shape and then hold a steam iron above the work. Do not iron the fabric directly, but allow the steam to sink into the fibres, then leave to dry.

Grandmother's garden

This is a reworking of a famous traditional patchwork block, producing a large piece made up entirely of hexagons and full of fond memories.

You will need:

- 800g (1lb 12oz) of crochet cotton no. 8 count (or 4-ply equivalent) in black
- 100g (3½oz) of crochet cotton no. 8 count (or 4-ply equivalent) in the following colours: pale pink, fuchsia, orange, burgundy, raspberry, old rose, green, coral, red, copper, dark khaki, apple green and rose
- 3.5mm hook

Sample

1 motif hexagonal
= 4.5 x 5.5cm
(1¾ x 2¼in)

Dimensions

See diagram

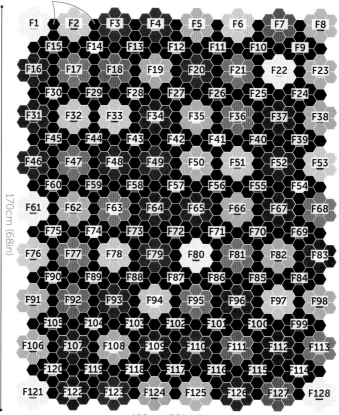

126cm (50½in)

170cm (68in)

To make

1. Start with a magic loop, then work the 7 hexagonal motifs required for 1 flower.

2. For colours, see Sequence of colours below.

Motif

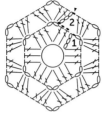

◄ Cut yarn

Assembly of a flower (F)

Sequence of colours

Filling	128 black motifs
F1	6 pale pink motifs, 1 apple green motif
F2	6 apple green motifs, 1 burgundy motif
F3	6 burgundy motifs, 1 green motif
F4	6 raspberry motifs, 1 orange motif
F5, F98, F106	6 orange motifs, 1 fuchsia motif
F6	6 old rose motifs, 1 green motif
F7	6 copper motifs, 1 pink motif
F8, F91	6 green motifs, 1 fuchsia motif
F9, F29, F40, F59,	6 black motifs, 1 burgundy motif
F10, F27, F39, F56, F69, F85, F101, F117	6 black motifs, 1 copper motif
F11, F24, F60	6 black motifs, 1 pink motif
F12, F75, F89, F103, F120	6 black motifs, 1 coral motif
F13, F73, F102	6 black motifs, 1 raspberry motif
F14, F41, F54, F74, F87	6 black motifs, 1 pale pink motif
F15, F44, F72, F100	6 black motifs, 1 dark khaki motif
F16	6 fuchsia motifs, 1 burgundy motif
F17	6 pink motifs, 1 dark khaki motif
F18	6 copper motifs, 1 red motif
F19, F108	6 coral motifs, 1 pale pink motif
F20, F79	6 burgundy motifs, 1 fuchsia motif
F21	6 dark khaki motifs, 1 apple green motif

F22	6 pale pink motifs, 1 old rose motif
F23	6 orange motifs, 1 apple green motif
F25, F86, F118	6 black motifs, 1 green motif
F26, F45, F55, F84, F115	6 black motifs, 1 red motif
F28, F104	6 black motifs, 1 orange motif
F30, F43, F57	6 black motifs, 1 old rose motif
F31, F112	6 fuchsia motifs, 1 raspberry motif
F32	6 apple green motifs, 1 raspberry motif
F33, F53	6 old rose motifs, 1 fuchsia motif
F34	6 fuchsia motifs, 1 green motif
F35	6 green motifs, 1 pale pink motif
F36, F81	6 pink motifs, 1 copper motif
F37	6 red motifs, 1 burgundy motif
F38	6 coral motifs, 1 pink motif
F42	6 black motifs, 1 apple green motif
F46	6 red motifs, 1 fuchsia motif
F47	6 dark khaki motifs, 1 pink motif
F48	6 raspberry motifs, 1 apple green motif
F49	6 burgundy motifs, 1 copper motif
F50	6 orange motifs, 1 pale pink motif
F51	6 apple green motifs, 1 copper motif
F52	6 raspberry motifs, 1 pink motif
F58, F70, F88, F99, F105, F116, F119	6 black motifs, 1 fuchsia motif
F61	6 pale pink motifs, 1 copper motif
F62	6 coral motifs, 1 dark khaki motif
F63	6 pink motifs, 1 pale pink motif
F64, F67	6 fuchsia motifs, 1 copper motif
F65	6 red motifs, 1 old rose motif
F66	6 green motifs, 1 burgundy motif
F68	6 dark khaki motifs, 1 apple green motif
F71, F90, F114	6 black motifs, 1 apple green motif

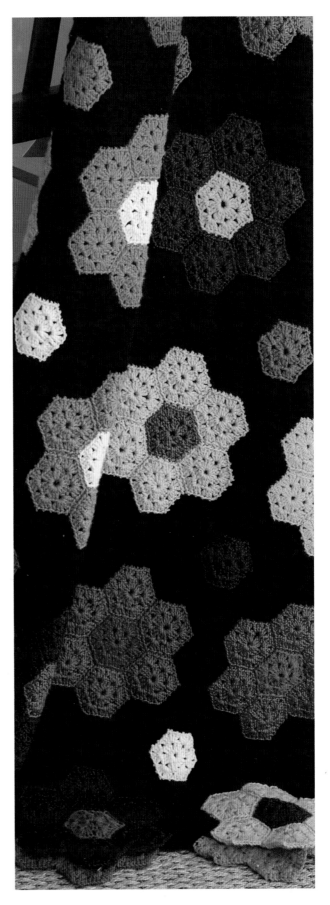

Sequence of colours

F76	6 apple green, 1 red
F77	6 pink, 1 raspberry
F78	6 old rose, 1 orange
F80	6 pale pink, 1 red
F82	6 coral, 1 raspberry
F83	6 fuchsia, 1 pale pink
F92	6 copper, 1 raspberry
F93	6 raspberry, 1 dark khaki
F94	6 apple green, 1 dark khaki
F95	6 pink, 1 coral
F96	6 red, 1 green
F97	6 old rose, 1 apple green
F107	6 red motifs, 1 raspberry motif
F109	6 fuchsia, 1 apple green
F110	6 burgundy, 1 coral
F111	6 copper, 1 apple green motif

F113	6 dark khaki, 1 orange
F121	6 pale pink, 1 dark khaki
F122	6 fuchsia, 1 orange
F123	6 burgundy, 1 old rose
F124	6 coral, 1 red
F125	6 green, 1 old rose
F126	6 raspberry, 1 old rose
F127	6 copper, 1 burgundy
F128	6 pale pink, 1 fuchsia

3. Assemble the motifs by oversewing (see Additonal methods) to create 1 flower using 6 motifs of the same colour and 1 central motif of another colour. Then assemble the flowers and use single hexagonals to fill in between the flowers by oversewing.

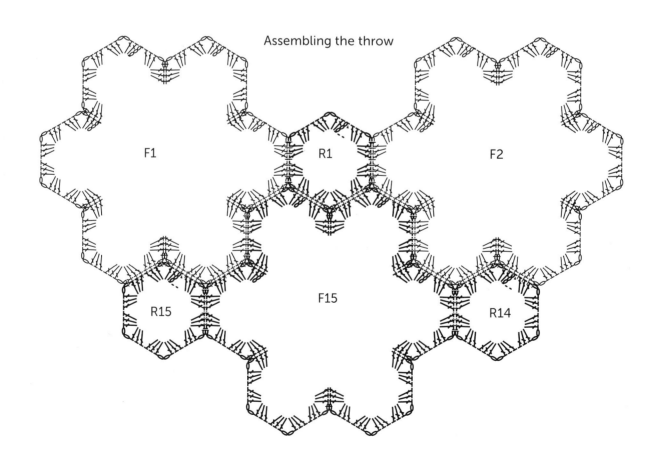

Assembling the throw

F1   R1   F2

R15   F15   R14

Open air log cabins

Play with contrast, place cool and warm shades next to each other and switch the traditional red in the centre for sky blue.

You will need:

- 100g (3½oz) of Rowan Felted Tweed DK yarn in the following colours: Cool: sky blue (**SB**), navy blue (**NB**), dark blue (**DB**), bottle green (**BGR**), blue-grey (**BG**), lime green (**LG**), beige (**BE**), blue (**B**), violet (**V**) and slate (**SL**). Warm: ecru (**E**), copper (**C**), gold (**G**), raspberry (**R**), old rose (**OR**), mauve (**M**) and brown (**BR**)
- 250g (9oz) of Rowan Felted Tweed yarn in raspberry (**R**)
- 3.5mm hook

Sample

1 motif = 22 x 22cm (8½ x 8½in)

Dimensions

See diagram

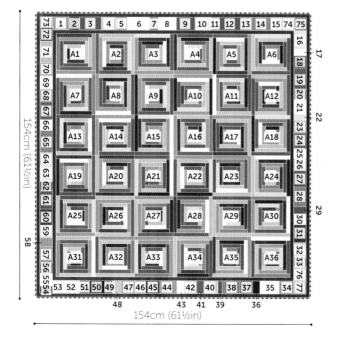

To make

1. Start with a magic loop and work the **A** motifs following the diagram below. For colours see Sequence of colours below.

Sequence of colours

For all **A** motifs, work rounds **1–3** in sky blue. Work rounds **4–5, 8–9, 12–13, 16–17, 20–21, 24–25, 28–29** and **32–33** in cool tones (NB, DB, BGR, LG, BE, B, V and SL) and rounds **6–7, 10–11, 14–15, 18–19, 22–23, 26–27, 30–31** and **34–35** in warm shades (BE, E, C, G, R, OR, M and BR), referring to the photo.

2. Assemble the throw with 6 rows of 6 motifs by oversewing (see Additional methods).

3. For the **internal border**, work 2 rounds of tr in raspberry. Then work 77 rectangles using a different number of trebles and working 8 rows, so the rectangles are various sizes. For colours, see Sequence of colours below, follow the numerical order on the diagram on page 38. Assemble all of the rectangles by oversewing (see diagram in Additional methods).

4. For the **outside border**, work 2 rounds of tr. and 1 round of shell stitch in raspberry as shown in the diagram.

Motif A

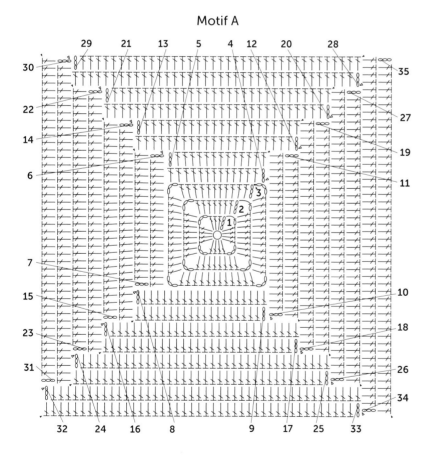

Sequence of colours

1, 11, 46	B
2, 18, 36, 50, 54, 62	NB
3, 12, 24, 39, 56	SL
4, 15, 32, 40, 64	BE
5, 14, 28, 33, 38, 65, 68	DB
6, 21, 25, 52, 66	LB
7, 19, 37, 41, 67	BR
8, 17, 35, 43, 55, 69	E
9, 20, 27, 51, 61	C
10, 16, 22, 30, 53, 63	LG
13, 47, 57, 73, 77	G
26, 42, 59, 71, 74	M
23, 34, 44, 58, 70	OR
31, 45, 60, 72, 75	V
29, 49	BGR
48, 76	BG

❖   See Additional methods for how to change colours

◄   Cut yarn   △   Attach yarn

Borders

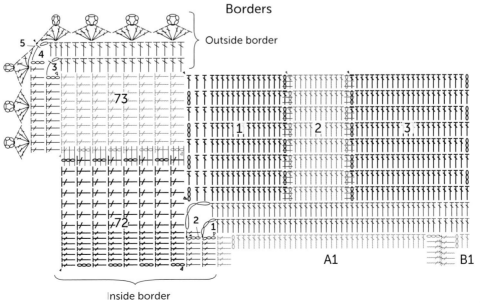

Outside border

73

72

Inside border

A1

B1

1, 2, 3...
sunshine!

Some carefully chosen printed fabrics for the centres, borders crocheted around for petals, a fill-in motif in various shades....that's all there is to it!

You will need:

- 100g (3½oz) of cotton in the following colours: ecru, beige, brown, orange, pink and black
- Assorted fabrics
- Fleece
- 3.5mm hook

Sample

1 fill-in motif = 22 x 22cm (8½ x 8½in)

Dimensions

See diagram

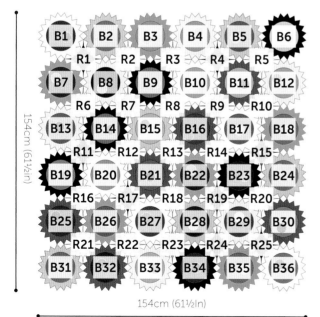

To make

1. Make a ring of 120 ch and join with a sl st. Work the **border** as shown in the diagram.

Sequence of colours – borders

B1,B10, B17, B20, B27, B36	ecru
B2, B5, B15, B24, B28, B31	beige
B3, B7, B18, B22, B26, B35	orange
B4, B8, B12, B13, B29, B33	pink
B6, B9, B14, B19, B23, B34	black
B11, B16, B21, B25, B30, B32	brown

2. Make 36 borders (for colours, see Sequence of colours – borders, opposite). Starting from the 2nd border, attach to the previous border with slip stitches as shown in the diagram. Make 6 rows of 6 borders.

3. Make 25 **fill-in motifs** (for colours, see Sequence of colours – motifs on page 46). When working the last round of the motif, join the piece to the borders using slip stitches, as shown in the **Fill-in motif** diagram (see page 46).

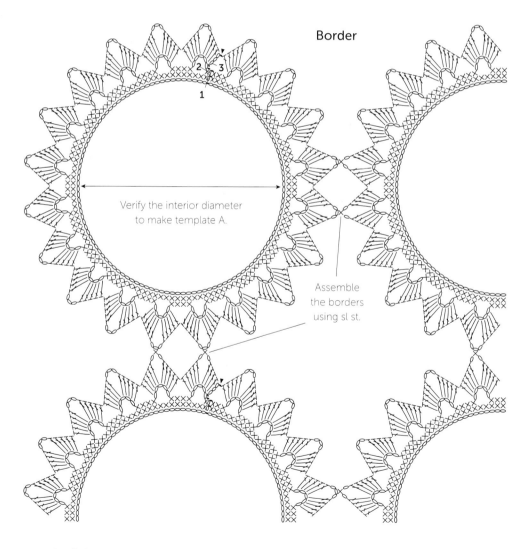

Border

Verify the interior diameter to make template A.

Assemble the borders using sl st.

◄ Cut yarn

Sequence of colours – motifs

R2, R5, R13, R20, R21	ecru
R3, R6, R10, R14, R22	beige
R7, R9, R23	orange
R8, R12, R16, R18	pink
R1, R4, R17, R25	black
R11, R15, R19, R24	brown

4. Check the interior diameter of the circles of the border pieces and prepare **template A** to cut out the fabric as follows:

Make the fabric circles

Use **template A** to cut 72 circles of different fabric, adding a seam allowance of 1cm (½in).

Cut out **template A** 36 times in fleece, adding a seam allowance of 0.5cm (¼in).

Place 2 fabric circles right sides together and place the fleece circle on top. Sew around the edges, leaving a gap of around 5cm (2in).
Turn the work through this opening, so the fleece is now on the inside of the circle. Close the gap with invisible stitches.

5. Sew the circles into the centre of each border using invisible stitches.

Fill-in motif

Nine squares with flowers in relief

With its palette of flashy colours and its small flowers, this throw evokes the atmosphere of the sixties and seventies.

You will need:

- 50g (1¾oz) of cotton in the following colours: dark blue, fuchsia, pink, coral, ecru and dark red
- 100g (3½oz) of cotton in the following colours: light blue, turquoise, sky blue, red and lime green
- 3.5mm hook

Sample

1 motif B = 16.5 x 16.5cm (6½ x 6½in)

Dimensions

See diagram

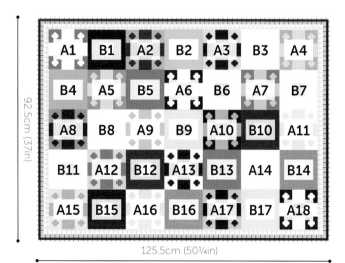

To make

1. Start by making a magic loop and work the motifs **a1** and **a2** for the nine patch square **A** as shown in the diagrams. For colour changes, see Sequence of colours – motif A, right.

Motif a1

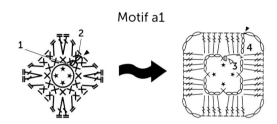

Work the double crochets of the 3rd round in the back loop left free by the double crochets of the 2nd round.

Motif a2

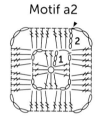

❖ See Additional methods for how to change colours

Ŧ Ŧ x̄ **Relief stitch:** work the stitch (dc, htr or tr) in the FRONT loop of the stitches in the previous round.

2. Assemble the **a1** and **a2** motifs in an alternating manner, oversewing them together (see Additional methods).

Motif A

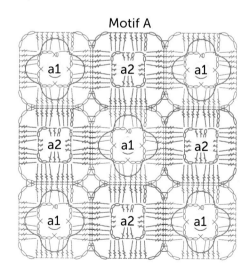

3. Work the **B** motifs.

Sequence of colours - motif A

	Motifs a1	Motifs a2
A1	1st–2nd rnd: sky blue 3rd–4th rnd: dark blue	sky blue
A2	1st–2nd rnd: dark red 3rd–4th rnd: red	dark red
A3	1st–2nd rnd: red 3rd–4th rnd: lime green	red
A4	1st–2nd rnd: lime green 3rd–4th rnd: pink	lime green
A5	1st–2nd rnd: lime green 3rd–4th rnd: coral	lime green
A6	1st–2nd rnd: ecru 3rd–4th rnd: fuchsia	ecru
A7	1st–2nd rnd: turquoise 3rd–4th rnd: dark blue	turquoise
A8	1st–2nd rnd: rouge 3rd–4th rnd: coral	rouge
A9	1st–2nd rnd: turquoise 3rd–4th rnd: light blue	turquoise
A10	1st–2nd rnd: pink 3rd–4th rnd: fuchsia	pink
A11	1st–2nd rnd: lime green 3rd–4th rnd: light blue	lime green
A12	1st–2nd rnd: dark blue 3rd–4th rnd: lime green	dark blue
A13	1st–2nd rnd: red 3rd–4th rnd: light blue	red
A14	1st–2nd rnd: pink 3rd–4th rnd: lime green	ecru
A15	1st–2nd rnd: pink 3rd–4th rnd: lime green	pink
A16	1st–2nd rnd: lime green 3rd–4th rnd: light blue	lime green
A17	1st–2nd rnd: fuchsia 3rd–4th rnd: turquoise	fuchsia
A18	1st–2nd rnd: light blue 3rd–4th rnd: red	red

Motif B

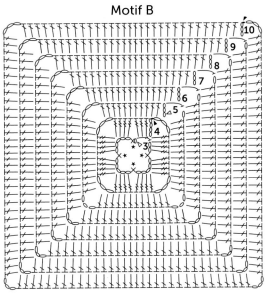

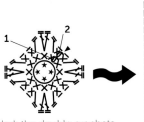

Work the double crochets
of the 3rd round in the
back loop left free by the
double crochets of
the 2nd round.

◀   Cut yarn

△   Attach yarn

Relief stitch: work the
stitch (dc, htr or tr) in
only the FRONT loop of
the stitch in the previous
round.

Sequence of colours - motif B

	1st–2nd rnd	3rd–4th rnd	5th–10th rnd
B1	coral	light blue	fuchsia
B2	dark blue	lime green	turquoise
B3	red	lime green	light blue
B4	turquoise	lime green	pink
B5	red	lime green	dark blue
B6	light blue	dark red	light blue
B7	red	fuchsia	ecru
B8	pink	lime green	ecru
B9	red	dark blue	lime green
B10	lime green	dark blue	dark red
B11	coral	fuchsia	light blue
B12	lime green	light blue	dark red
B13	dark red	coral	dark blue
B14	dark blue	ecru	coral
B15	dark blue	ecru	red

B16	fuchsia	ecru	coral
B17	lime green	coral	lime green

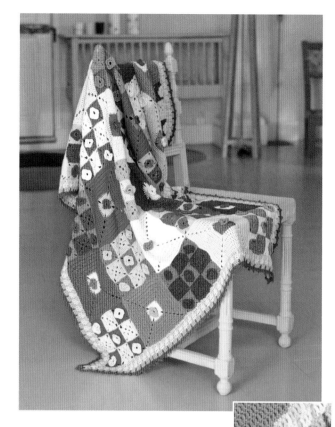

4. Assemble the **A** and **B** motifs in an alternating manner, using invisible stitches (see Additional methods).

5. For the **border**, work 2 rounds in lime green, 2 rounds in sky blue, 2 rounds in turquoise and 2 rounds in red, as shown in the diagram opposite.

Assembly

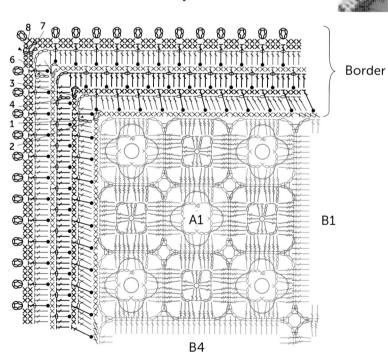

Work the tr in the corresponding stitch of the round before last and on top of the chain stitch of the previous round.

Round the world

This gorgeous giant bedspread is made up of a flower crocheted 441 times, in shades ranging from pale pink to violet.

You will need:

- 100% merino yarn (125m; 410ft/50g; 1¾oz) in the following colours: 50g (1¾oz) of pink (**P**), 100g (3½oz) of old rose (**OR**), 150g (5½oz) of beige (**BE**), 150g (5½oz)of brown (**BR**), 200g (7oz) of coral (**C**), 200g (7oz) of red (**RO**), 300g (10½oz) of dark red (**DR**), 300g (10½oz) of fuchsia (**F**), 350g (12½oz) of burgundy (**B**), 400g (14oz) of violet (**V**), 400g (14oz) of blackberry (**BB**) and 100g (3½oz) of mauve (**M**)
- 3.5mm hook

Sample

1 motif = 8 x 8cm (3 x 3in)

Dimensions

See diagram

R	VR	BE	M	C	RO	RF	F	B	V	MU	V	B	F	RF	RO	C	M	BE	VR	R
VR	BE	M	C	RO	RF	F	B	V	MU	V	MU	V	B	F	RF	RO	C	M	BE	VR
BE	M	C	RO	RF	F	B	V	MU	V	B	V	MU	V	B	F	RF	RO	C	M	BE
M	C	RO	RF	F	B	V	MU	V	B	F	B	V	MU	V	B	F	RF	RO	C	M
C	RO	RF	F	B	V	MU	V	B	F	RF	F	B	V	MU	V	B	F	RF	RO	C
RO	RF	F	B	V	MU	V	B	F	RF	RO	RF	F	B	V	MU	V	B	F	RF	RO
RF	F	B	V	MU	V	B	F	RF	RO	C	RO	RF	F	B	V	MU	V	B	F	RF
F	B	V	MU	V	B	F	RF	RO	C	M	C	RO	RF	F	B	V	MU	V	B	F
B	V	MU	V	B	F	RF	RO	C	M	BE	M	C	RO	RF	F	B	V	MU	V	B
V	MU	V	B	F	RF	RO	C	M	BE	VR	BE	M	C	RO	RF	F	B	V	MU	V
MU	V	B	F	RF	RO	C	M	BE	VR	R	VR	BE	M	C	RO	RF	F	B	V	MU
V	MU	V	B	F	RF	RO	C	M	BE	VR	BE	M	C	RO	RF	F	B	V	MU	V
B	V	MU	V	B	F	RF	RO	C	M	BE	M	C	RO	RF	F	B	V	MU	V	B
F	B	V	MU	V	B	F	RF	RO	C	M	C	RO	RF	F	B	V	MU	V	B	F
RF	F	B	V	MU	V	B	F	RF	RO	C	RO	RF	F	B	V	MU	V	B	F	RF
RO	RF	F	B	V	MU	V	B	F	RF	RO	RF	F	B	V	MU	V	B	F	RF	RO
C	RO	RF	F	B	V	MU	V	B	F	RF	F	B	V	MU	V	B	F	RF	RO	C
M	C	RO	RF	F	B	V	MU	V	B	F	B	V	MU	V	B	F	RF	RO	C	M
BE	M	C	RO	RF	F	B	V	MU	V	B	V	MU	V	B	F	RF	RO	C	M	BE
VR	BE	M	C	RO	RF	F	B	V	MU	V	MU	V	B	F	RF	RO	C	M	BE	VR
V	VR	BE	M	C	RO	RF	F	B	V	MU	V	B	F	RF	RO	C	M	BE	VR	V

176cm (70in)

176cm (70in)

To make

1. Start with a ring of 8 ch, joined with a slip stitch. Then crochet the motif following the diagram below.

2. For Sequence of colours, see diagram on page 54.

3. Starting from the 2nd motif, join to the previous motif as shown in the diagram below. Make 441 motifs joining them in 21 rows of 21 motifs.

4. For the **border**, work 1 round of dc and ch and 1 round of tr in mauve, 1 round of tr and 1 round of shells in blackberry, as shown in the diagram below.

Assembly

Border

Motif

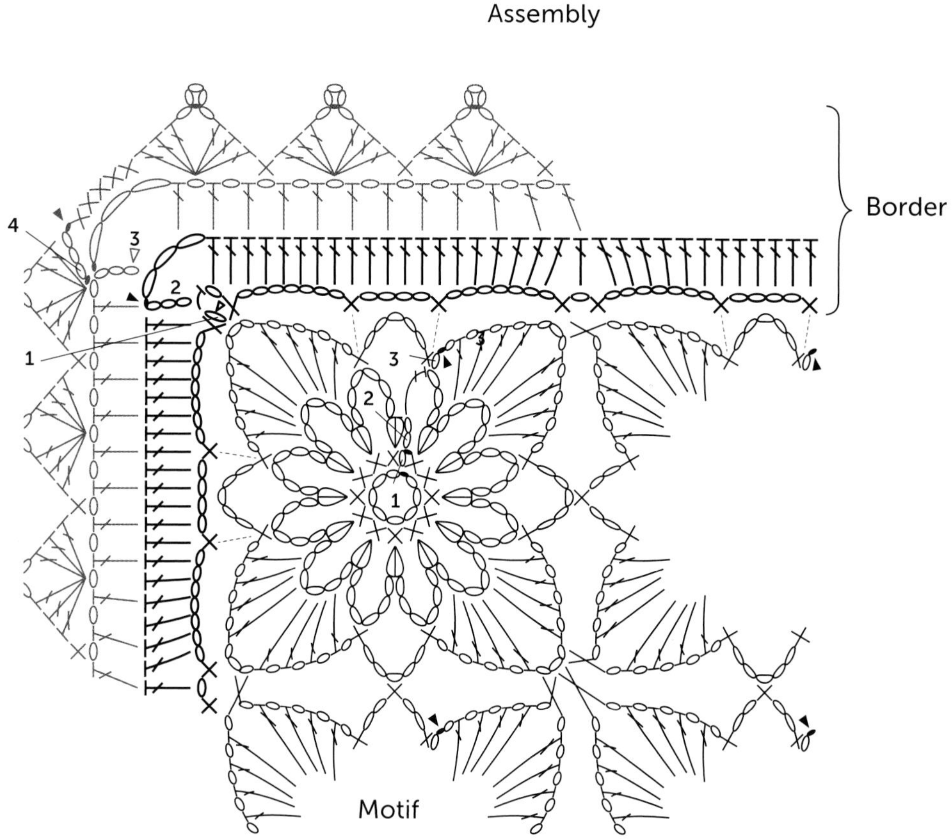

◀ Cut yarn   ◁ Attach yarn

⍭ **Puff stitch**: *Yarn over once, insert the hook in the stitch, yarn over once, pull yarn through the stitch *, repeat 3 times in the same stitch, yarn over once, pull yarn through all the loops on the hook

Hexagon mosaic

Like a scrap quilt, this piece is all about the variety of colours which have a surprise element as they come together, yet the pattern creates an overall harmony.

You will need:

- 50g (1¾oz) of Rowan Fine Tweed yarn in the 23 different colours available in the range
- 3.5mm hook

Sample

1 motif = 15 x 18.5cm (6 x 7¼in)

Dimensions

See diagram

242cm (96¾in)

141cm (56¼in)

To make

1. Start with a ring of 6 ch joined with a slip stitch. Then crochet the motif following the diagram below.

2. Make 81 motifs, changing colours randomly through the work. Don't use more than four colours in each motif.

Motif

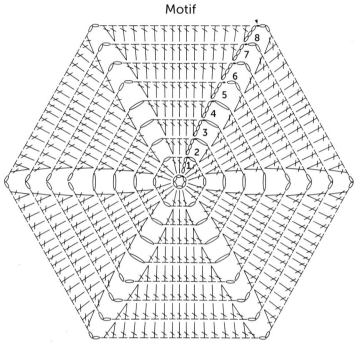

❖   See Additonal methods for how to change colours

◀   Cut yarn   △   Attach yarn

3. Assemble the motifs by oversewing (see Additional methods).

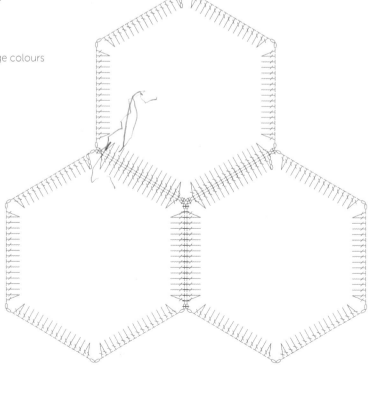

Assembly

Bright colours for kids

This variation on the hexagon includes 50 different shades arranged in stages, surrounded by yellow and green lollipop colours.

You will need:

- 50 skeins of DMC Soft Cotton no.89 in many different colours
- DMC Natura Cotton Thread in the following colours: 100g (3½oz) of no.02 (ivory), 100g (3½oz) of no.76 (bamboo) and 150g (5½oz) in no.16 (sunflower)
- 3mm hook

Sample

1 motif = 10 x 11.5cm (4 x 4½in)

Dimensions

See diagram

To make

1. Start with a ring of 6 ch, joined with a slip stitch. Then crochet the motif following the diagram opposite.

2. Make 50 motifs, for colours see Sequence of colours below.

Sequence of colours

1st rnd	ivory
2nd–3rd rnd	choice of soft cotton
4th rnd	ivory
5th rnd	sunflower
6th rnd	bamboo

3. Assemble the motifs in 9 rows of 6 or 5 motifs, by oversewing (see Additonal methods), as shown in the **assembly** diagram.

4. For the **border,** work 1 round of tr in green and 1 round of tr with popcorn stitch in yellow, as shown in the diagram.

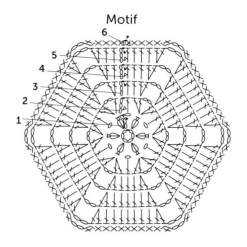

Motif

❖   See Additional methods for how to change colours

◀   Cut yarn   △   Attach yarn

⬙   **Puff stitch**: *Yarn over once, insert the hook in the stitch, yarn over once, pull yarn through the stitch *, repeat 3 times in the same stitch, yarn over once, pull yarn through all the loops on the hook

⤸   Work 2 double crochet in the same stitch

⬗   4 ch, 1 **popcorn stitch** with 6 trebles: stretch the loop a little from the hook and take it out of the work, then insert it from front to back in the top of the 1st of 6 trebles, pick up the loop and pull it through the stitch, Then work 4 ch and 1 slip stitch in th 1st ch.

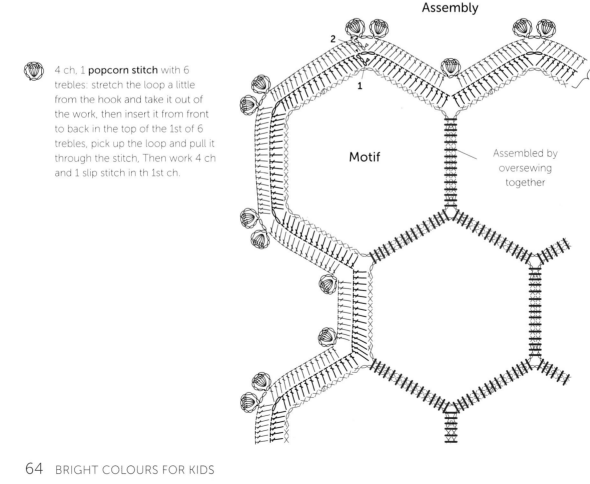

Assembly

Border

Motif

Assembled by oversewing together

Fans

Using a combination of blue and brown, softened by beige and ecru, this small, light throw is bordered with picots.

You will need:

- 100g (3½oz) of Katia 100% linen in the following colours: navy blue, dark blue, blue-grey, ecru, beige, dark beige, brown
- 3.5mm hook

Sample

1 motif **A** = 14.5 x 14.5cm (5¾ x 5¾in)

Dimensions

See diagram

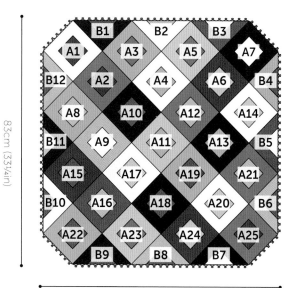

83cm (33¼in)

83cm (33¼in)

To make

1. Start with a ring of 6 ch. joined with a slip stitch. Then crochet **motif A**, following the diagram below. Start the second colour in round 6, alternating colour choices throughout.

Motif A

❖   See Additional methods for how to change colours

◀   Cut yarn   △   Attach yarn

3. Make 12 **B motifs**, following the diagram below, and join them as you go to the **A motifs** in the last round with sl st.

4. For the **border**, follow the instructions in the diagram at the bottom of the page.

Motif B

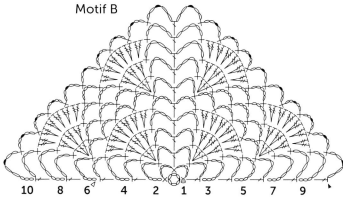

Sequence of colours

1st–5th round or row	colour 1 of your choice
6th–10th round or row	colour 2 of your choice

2. Work **motif A** 25 times, attaching each motif to the previous ones, using double crochet as shown in the diagram, right. Follow the numerical order A1 to A25 in the diagram on page 66.

◀ Cut yarn

△ Attach yarn

🌼 **Picot:** 5 ch., work 1 sl st in the 1st ch.

Assembly

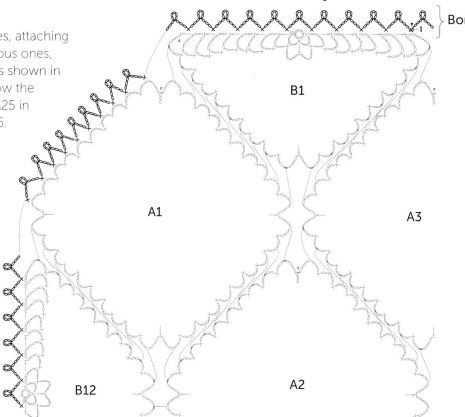

Tutti-frutti grannies

With fruity red, mint or orange tones, these cushions in multiple shades will give sofas and armchairs a new lease of life and brighten up your living space.

GENERAL FEATURES OF ALL FOUR CUSHIONS

Sample

1st–3rd rounds. = 6.5 x 6.5cm (15¼ x 15¼in)

To make

1. Start with a magic loop and work following the diagram below. Change the colour as specified for each cushion (see Sequence of colours).

2. For the **border**, work 1 round of tr in black, 1 round of dc in red and 1 round of tr in black as shown in the diagram below.

3. Create an envelope of fabric (see How to make a cushion cover) and sew on the crocheted part with invisible stitches.

CUSHION IN SHADES OF ORANGE AND VIOLET

You will need:

- Leftover yarn in the following colours: pink/orange, raspberry, plum, dark violet, dark plum, blackberry, violet, black and red
- 45 x 110cm (18 x44in) of assorted fabrics
- 3.5mm hook

Dimensions

See diagram

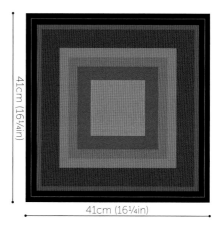

41cm (16¼in)

41cm (16¼in)

Sequence of colours

1st–6th rnd	pink/orange
7th–9th rnd	raspberry
10th–11th rnd	plum
12th–13th rnd	dark violet
14th–15th rnd	dark plum
16th–18th rnd	blackberry
19th rnd	violet

❖   See Additional Methods for how to change colours

◀   Cut yarn

◁   Attach yarn

↭   Work 2 double crochet in the same stitch

3 2   1st round of border

4
3
2
1

The number of rounds differs depending on the cushion.

CUSHION IN SHADES OF BLUE AND GREEN

You will need:

- Leftover yarn in the following colours: light blue, blue-green, green, bottle green, khaki, mid-green, lime green, black and red
- 50 x 110cm (20 x 44in) of assorted fabric 3.5mm hook

Dimensions

See diagram

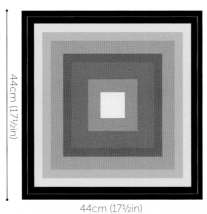

44cm (17½in)

44cm (17½in)

Sequence of colours

1st–3rd rnds.	light blue
4th–7th rnd	blue-green
8th–12th rnd	green
13th–14th rnd	bottle green
15th–17th rnd	khaki
18th–19th rnd	mid-green
20th–21st rnd	lime green

CUSHION IN SHADES OF VIOLET AND BLUE

You will need:

- Leftover yarn in the following colours: violet, slate, navy blue, blue, light blue, black and red
- 45 x 110cm (18 x 44in) of assorted fabrics
- 3.5mm hook

Dimensions

See diagram

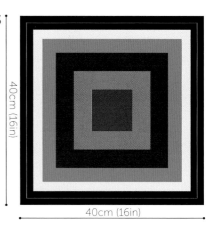

40cm (16in)

40cm (16in)

Sequence of colours

1st–6th rnd	violet
7th–9th rnd	slate
10th–14th rnd	navy blue
15th–17th rnd	blue
18th–19th rnd	light blue

CUSHION IN SHADES OF BEIGE, GREEN AND ORANGE

You will need:

- Leftover yarn in the following colours: pale yellow, beige, green-beige, khaki-beige, yellow, orange, coral, brown, black and red
- 60 x 120cm (24 x 48in) of assorted fabrics
- 3.5mm hook

Dimensions

See diagram

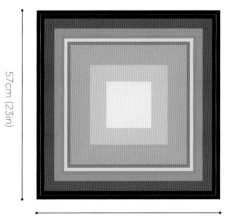

57cm (23in)

57cm (23in)

Sequence of colours

1st–10th rnd	pale yellow
11th–14th rnd	beige
15th–17th rnd	green-beige
18th–20th rnd	khaki-beige
21st round	yellow
22nd rnd	orange
23rd–24th rnd	coral
25th–27th rnd	brown

Variation on fans

Here is a great opportunity to use up your leftover yarn and try some daring colour combinations.

You will need:

- Leftover yarn in the following colours: old rose, midnight blue, bright orange, lime green, pale green, mustard, raspberry, plum and blue
- 60 x 120cm (24 x 48in) of assorted fabrics
- 3.5mm hook

Sample

1 motif = 24.5 x 24.5cm (10 x 10in)

Dimensions

See diagram

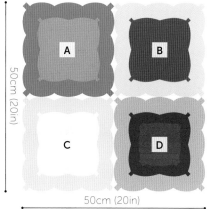

To make

1. Start with a ring of 6 ch joined with a slip stitch. Then work the **motif** following the diagram, right.

2. For colour changes, see Sequence of colours.

3. Work the second, third and forth motifs following the chart, attaching them to the previous motifs with slip stitches, as shown in the **assembly** diagram below.

4. Create an envelope of fabric (see How to make a cushion cover) and sew on the crocheted part with invisible stitches.

❖   See Additional methods for how to change colours

◀ Cut yarn   △ Attach yarn

Motif

Assembly

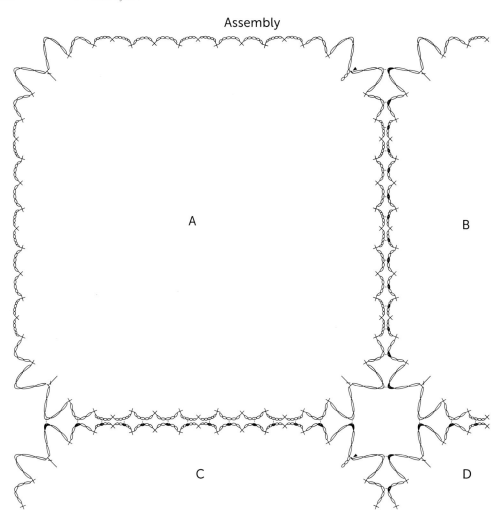

A   B

C   D

Sequence of colours

	Motif A	Motif B	Motif C		Motif D
1st–10th rnd	old rose	bright orange	pale green	1st–6th rnd	raspberry
11th–14th rnd	midnight blue	lime green	mustard	7th–10th rnd	plum
				11th–14th rnd	blue

Bohemian

This cosy cushion is made by joining four granny squares – it couldn't be easier!

You will need:

- Leftover yarn in the following colours: beige, coral, violet, sea green, pink-red, blue, bottle green, brown, old rose, sky blue, mustard, bright orange, khaki, raspberry, midnight blue, yellow, dark beige and plum
- 45 x 110cm (18 x 44in) of assorted fabrics
- 3.5mm hook

Sample

1 motif =
17.5 x 17.5cm (7 x 7in)

Dimensions

See diagram

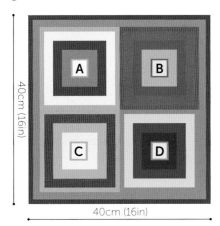

To make

1. Start with a magic loop and work the motif following the diagram above, right.

2. For colour changes, see Sequence of colours. Make the 4 motifs.

3. On the wrong side of the work, join motif **A** to motif **B** with one row of dc. Do the same with motifs **C** and **D**. Then join motifs **A/B** to motifs **C/D** using the same method.

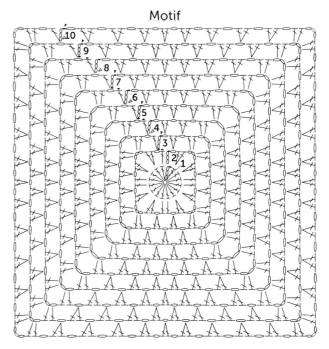

Motif

❖　See Additional methods for how to change colours

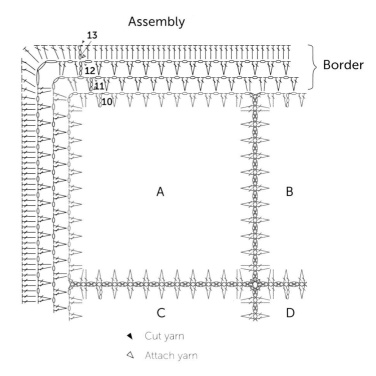

Assembly

Border

◀　Cut yarn
◁　Attach yarn

4. For the **border**, work 2 rnds in dark beige and 1 rnd of tr in plum, as shown in the diagram above.

5. Create an envelope of fabric (see How to make a cushion cover) and sew on the crocheted part with invisible stitches.

Sequence of colours

	Motif A	Motif B
1st–3rd rnd	beige	pink-red
4th–5th rnd	coral	blue
6th–7th rnd	violet	bottle green
8th–9th rnd	sea green	brown
10th rnd	beige	pink-red

	Motif C	Motif D
1st–3rd rnd	old rose	khaki
4th–5th rnd	sky blue	raspberry
6th–7th rnd	mustard	midnight blue
8th–9th rnd	bright orange	yellow
10th rnd	old rose	khaki

Light and shade

A subtle interplay of negative and positive lines, intriguing, captivating...built around a very simple flower in the centre.

You will need:

- 50g (1¾oz) of cotton in the following colours: pale pink, dark purple, violet, plum and black
- 45 x 110cm (18 x 44in) of assorted fabrics
- 3.5mm hook

Sample

1st–3rd round = 7 x 7cm (2¾ x 2¾in)

Dimensions

See diagram

40cm (16in)

40cm (16in)

To make

1. Start with a magic loop and work the motif following the diagram below. Note: starting from the 6th row, split the work in two, work from the 6th to the 21st round back and forth. Then complete the other half with the colours reversed.

2. For colour changes, see Sequence of colours below.

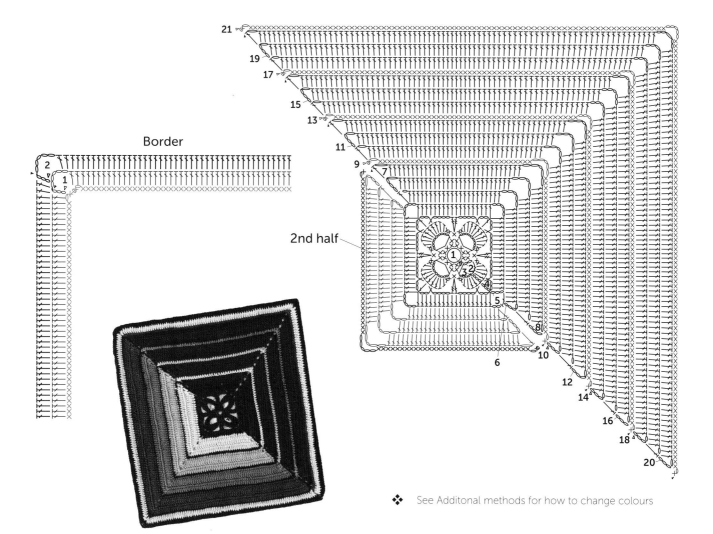

Border

2nd half

❖ See Additonal methods for how to change colours

Sequence of colours

1st–5th row	black
6th–8th row	half black, half pale pink
9th row	half pale pink, half black
10th–12th row	half black, half purple
13th row	half purple, half black
14th–16th row	half black, half violet
17th row	half violet, half black
18th–20th row	half black, half plum
21st row	half plum, half black

3. Join the two halves by oversewing (see Additional methods).

4. For the **border**, work 1 round of tr in pale pink and 1 round of tr in black, as shown on the diagram above, left.

5. Create an envelope of fabric (see How to make a cushion cover) and sew on the crocheted part with invisible stitches.

Shaded squares

In the same shades as the previous cushion, this cushion is both different and complementary.

You will need:

- 50g (1¾oz) of cotton in the following colours: pale pink, purple, violet, plum and black
- 45 x 110cm (18 x 44in) of assorted fabrics
- 3.5mm hook

Sample

1 motif = 14 x 14cm (5½ x 5½in)

Dimensions

See diagram

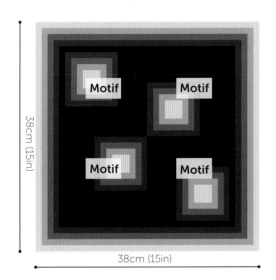

To make

1. Start with a magic loop and work the motif following the diagram top right.

2. For colour changes, see Sequence of colours. Make 4 identical motifs.

Motif

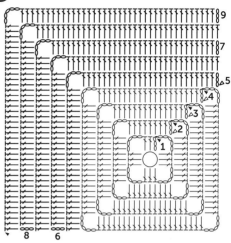

Sequence of colours

1st rnd	pale pink
2nd rnd	purple
3rd rnd	violet
4th rnd	plum
5th–9th row (on 2 sides)	black

3. Join the motifs together by oversewing (see Additional methods) in black.

4. For the **border**, work 1 round of tr in black, 1 round of tr in plum, 1 round of tr in violet, 1 round of tr in purple and 1 round of tr in pale pink, as shown in the diagram below.

5. Create an envelope of fabric (see How to make a cushion cover) and sew on the crocheted part with invisible stitches.

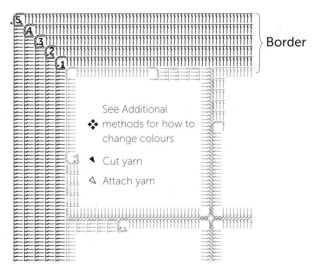

Border

❖ See Additional methods for how to change colours

◀ Cut yarn

◁ Attach yarn

Nine squares and flowers in relief

Based on the same principle as the Nine squares and flowers in relief throw, this bright and beautiful cushion has major impact because of the unexpected colour combinations.

You will need:

- Leftover yarn in the following colours: fuchsia, royal blue, orange, red, raspberry, plum, mustard, copper, lime green, green and black
- 60 x 120cm (24 x 48in) of assorted fabrics
- 3.5mm hook

Sample

1 motif B = 16.5 x 16.5cm (6¼ x 6¼in)

Dimensions

See diagram

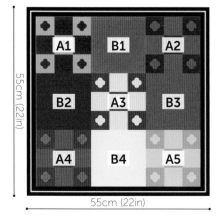

To make

1. Start by making a magic loop and work the motifs **a1** and **a2** for motif **A** as shown in diagrams. For colour changes, see Sequence of colours below.

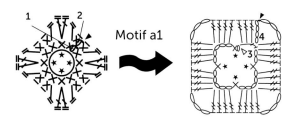

Motif a1

Work the double crochets of the 3rd round in the back loop left free by the double crochets of the 2nd round.

Motif a2

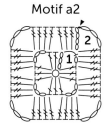

❖ See Additional methods for how to change colours

Sequence of colours - motif A

	a1	a2
A1	1st–2nd rnd: fuchsia 3rd–4th rnd: royal blue	fuchsia
A2	1st–2nd rnd: red 3rd–4th rnd: fuchsia	red
A3	1st–2nd rnd: mustard 3rd–4th rnd: plum	mustard
A4	1st–2nd rnd: orange 3rd–4th rnd: plum	copper
A5	1st–2nd rnd: green 3rd–4th rnd: copper	green

2. Join motifs **a1** and **a2** by oversewing (see Additional methods).

Motif A

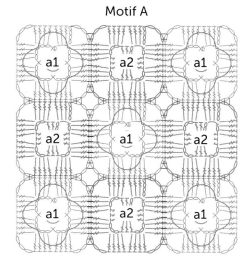

◀ Cut yarn   △ Attach yarn

Relief stitch: work the stitch (dc, htr, or tr) in the FRONT loop of the stitch in the previous round.

Sequence of colours - motif B

B1	1s–2nd rnd: mustard 3rd–10th rnd: orange
B2	1st–2nd rnd: red 3rd–10th rnd: raspberry
B3	1st–2nd rnd: plum 3rd–10th rnd: copper
B4	1st–2nd rnd: fuchsia 3rd–10th rnd: lime green

3. Work 4 **B** motifs, referring to the table above for colours.

4. Join motifs **A** and **B** oversewing (see Additional methods).

5. For the **border**, work 1 round of tr in black, 1 round of dc in mustard and 1 round of tr, as shown in the diagram opposite.

6. Create an envelope of fabric (see How to make a cushion cover) and sew on the crocheted part with invisible stitches.

Motif B

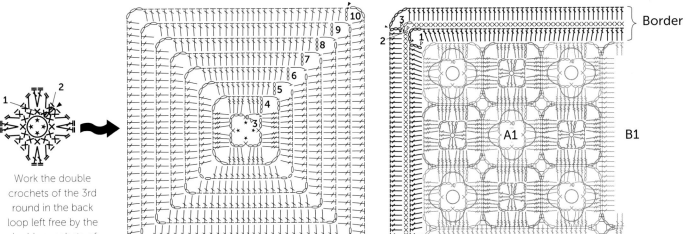

Work the double crochets of the 3rd round in the back loop left free by the double crochets of the 2nd round.

Border

A1

B1

B2

Stripes

Get all your yarn out of the cupboard and crochet some coloured stripes with this pretty daisy stitch. Vintage effect guaranteed!

You will need:

- Leftover yarn in the following colours: raspberry, off white, bottle green, dark red, fuchsia, midnight blue, purple, red, blue-grey, beige, khaki, old rose, lime green, sky blue, brown, copper, dark purple, plum, pink, blue-green, yellow, dark brown, light blue, orange, bright blue-green, burgundy, blue, green, lime green, mustard and black
- 60 x 120cm (24 x 48in) of assorted fabrics
- 3.5mm hook

Sample

1 motif = 16 x 16cm (6¼ x 6¼in)

Dimensions

See diagram

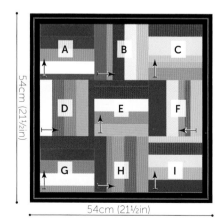

54cm (21½in)

54cm (21½in)

→ Direction of work

90

To make

1. Start with a base chain of 31 ch then work the motif following the diagram below and the instructions for daisy stitch.

Motif

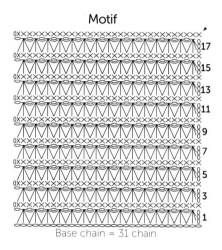

Base chain = 31 chain

❖ See Additional methods for how to change colours

Daisy stitch: 3 ch to turn the work, insert hook in the 2nd ch, yarn over once, pull yarn through the stitch, insert hook in the 3rd ch, yarn over once, pull yarn through the stitch, insert hook in the 4th ch, yarn over once, pull yarn through the stitch and insert hook in the 5th ch, yarn over once, pull yarn through the stitch – you should have 5 loops on the hook. Yarn over once and pull yarn through all 5 loops, then ch 1.
Insert the hook into the last ch 1 you made, yarn over once, pull through the stitch. Insert hook into the side of the stitch of the previous daisy (under both loops), yarn over once and pull through. Then insert hook into the next chain on the foundation chain, pull yarn through, and repeat into the next chain. You should have 5 loops on the hook. Yarn over once and pull yarn through all 5 loops on the hook, and ch 1.
Repeat from * to * for the rest of the row.

2. For colour changes, see Sequence of colours.

3. Make all 6 motifs.

Sequence of colours

	A
1st–2nd row	raspberry
3rd–6th row	off-white
7th–10th row	bottle green
11th–14th row	dark red
15th–18th row	fuchsia

	B
1st–4th row	midnight blue
5th–6th row	purple
7th–10th row	burgundy
11th–14th row	blue-grey
15th–18th row	beige

	C
1st–4th row	purple
5th–6th row	khaki
7th–8th row	old rose
9th–14th row	lime green
15th–18th row	raspberry

	D
1st–4th row	sky blue
5th–8th row	brown
9th–12th row	copper
13th–16th row	dark purple
17th–18th row	plum

	E
1st–4th row	pink
5th–8th row	blue-green
9th–12th row	yellow
13th–16th row	dark brown
17th–18th row	red

	F
1st–4th row	old rose
5th–6th row	orange
7th–10th row	bottle green
9th–12th row	light blue
13th–18th row	plum

	G
1st–2nd row	bottle green
3rd–6th row	lime green
7th–10th row	bright blue-green
11th–14th row	fuchsia
15th–16th row	plum
17th–18th row	burgundy

	H
1st–4th row	plum
5th–6th row	copper
7th–10th row	blue
11th–14th row	brown
15th–18th row	bottle green

	I
1st–4th row	plum
5th–8th row	off-white
9th–12th row	brown
13th–16th row	green
17th–18th row	mustard

3. Join the 3 x 3 motifs together by oversewing (see Additional methods) in 1 loop of each stitch.

4. For the **border**, work 2 rounds of tr in black, 1 round of dc in red, 2 rounds of tr in black, as shown in the diagram (right).

5. Create an envelope of fabric (see How to make a cushion cover) and sew on the crocheted part with invisible stitches.

Assembly

Border

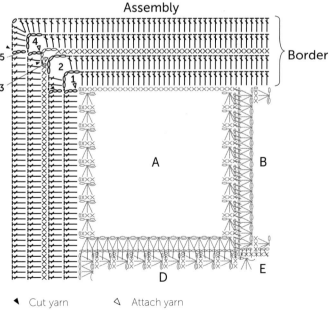

◄ Cut yarn   ◁ Attach yarn

Conversion charts

CROCHET TERMS

Be aware that crochet terms in the US are different from those in the UK. This can be confusing as the same terms are used to refer to different stitches under each system. The list here gives abbreviations and a translation of UK terms to US terms:

UK term	US term
single crochet	slip stitch
double crochet	single crochet
half treble	half double crochet
treble	double crochet
double treble	treble crochet
treble treble	double treble crochet

Crochet abbreviations

ss	slip stitch
st/es	stitch/es
ch	chain
ch-sp	chain space
sp	space
dc	double crochet
hdc	half double crochet
tr	treble
htr	half treble crochet
tr2tog	treble 2 together
sh	shell stitch
po	popcorn stitch
bldc	back loop double crochet
fan	fan stitch
v stitch	v stitch
yrh	yarn round hook
beg	beginning
rep	repeat
foll	following
sk	skip
ws	wrong side
rs	right side

Metric and imperial measurements

These patterns have been created using metric measurements. Although imperial measurements appear in brackets after each metric measurement, for best results we recommend using the metric measurements provided.

Crochet hook sizes

Crochet hooks come in a range of sizes, and the size of hook needed is directly related to the thickness of yarn being used. A fine yarn requires a small hook, while a thick yarn will need a much chunkier hook. There are two main sizing schemes for crochet hooks: the metric system (used in the UK and Europe) and the American system. The chart here lists the sizes available, with conversions for both systems.

Metric Sizes	American Sizes
2.00mm	B1
2.25mm	B1
2.50mm	C2
2.75mm	C2
3.00mm	D3
3.25mm	D3
3.50mm	E4
3.75mm	F5
4.00mm	G6
4.50mm	7
5.00mm	H8
5.50mm	I9
6.00mm	J10
6.50mm	K10½
7.00mm	-
8.00mm	L11
9.00mm	M/N13
10.00mm	N/P15
12.00mm	O16
15.00mm	P/Q
16.00mm	Q
19.00mm	S

Knitting needle sizes

Metric	Old UK	USA
2mm	14	0
2.25mm	13	1
2.5mm		
2.75mm	12	2
3mm	11	
3.25mm	10	3
3.5mm		4
3.75mm	9	5
4mm	8	6
4.5mm	7	7
5mm	6	8

Suppliers

Modern Knitting
www.modernknitting.co.uk
Tel: 01279 771153

Pack Lane Wool
www.packlanewool.co.uk
Tel: 01256 462590

RKM Wools
www.rkmwools.co.uk
Tel: 01743 245623

Rowan Yarns
www.knitrowan.com
Tel: 01484 681881

Sew and So
www.sewandso.co.uk
Tel: 0800 013 0150

Stitch Craft Create
www.stitchcraftcreate.co.uk
Tel: 0844 880 5851

Index

A DAVID & CHARLES BOOK
© Les Éditions De Saxe 2014
Originally published as Crochet Country

First published in the UK in 2014 by F&W Media International, Ltd
David & Charles is an imprint of F&W Media International, Ltd
Brunel House, Forde Close, Newton Abbot, TQ12 4PU, UK

F&W Media International, Ltd is a subsidiary of F+W Media, Inc
10151 Carver Road, Suite #200, Blue Ash, OH 45242, USA

A catalogue record for this book is available from the British
Library.

ISBN-13: 978-1-4463-0533-1 paperback
ISBN-10: 1-4463-0533-3 paperback

Printed in China by RR Donnelley for:
F&W Media International, Ltd
Brunel House, Forde Close, Newton Abbot, TQ12 4PU, UK

10 9 8 7 6 5 4 3 2 1
Designer: Kristel Salgarollo
Artistic director: Joanna Perraudin
Drawings and technical explanations: Céline Cantat
Photography: Pierre Nicou and Didier Barbecot
Stylist: Marie-Paule Faure
Acquisitions Editor (UK): Sarah Callard
Desk Editor (UK): Charlotte Andrew
Pattern Checker (UK): Caroline Voaden
Designer (UK): Jennifer Stanley
Senior Production Controller (UK): Beverley Richardson

F+W Media publishes high quality books on a wide range of
subjects.
For more great book ideas visit: www.stitchcraftcreate.co.uk